AF266859

Jan Laurens Siesling

Americana

&

One Day Jesus Christ

p o e t r y

just so **J!S** editions

Three attributes make the United States of America stand
out amidst the nations: democracy, guns and Jesus.
Their common trait is that they are all ill-used.
The first one is weakening into mythical proportions, so
that one wonders if it ever existed.
The last one is so overwhelmingly present, that she is
now as hollow as a decorated Easter egg.
In the middle stands the gun, he is real.

ISBN 978-1-0878-6375-7

To the Fathers

Table

AMERICANA

Guns 'n Prayers

I.

it was a summer day
it was a windy day
it was a normal day
it was a fun day
it was gunday

it was a warm day
it was a winter day
it was a long day
it was a special day
it was gunday

gunday it was
seven gundays in the week
thirty in the month
three hundred in the year
gunday every day

gunday in school
gunday in church
gunday in the theater
gunday in the mall
gunday in america

II.

so the father prayed
so the mother prayed
so the sister prayed
so the brother prayed
so the family prayed

the pastor prayed
the mayor prayed
the governor prayed
the senator prayed
congress prayed

the president prayed
the first lady prayed
the vp prayed
the wife of the vp prayed
the white house prayed

the black people prayed
the white people prayed
the red people prayed
the yellow people prayed
the brown people prayed

the teacher prayed
the principal prayed
the football coach prayed
the bus driver prayed
the policeman prayed

the dog prayed
the cat prayed
the horse prayed
the ass prayed
the oxen prayed

the quarterback prayed
the singer prayed
the porn star prayed
the millionaire prayed
the homeless prayed

the doctor prayed
the sheriff prayed
the rifle club owner prayed
the gun shop owner prayed
the gunman prayed

god bless america
in god we trust
god created the gun
one nation under the gun
god save the gun

III.

god of course heard it all
he couldn't sleep
and he said jesus!
what's that noise
all day and all of the night

jesus then said my god they pray
they have fun
they have a gun
and as i often say
no gun no pray

gee, don't speak in rhyme
to me that hurts my ears
have mercy and go tell
them they could as well
(hmm) go to hell, no rhyme intended

so jesus became the lord
if you hadn't heard
with slippers blue eyes and a beard
he descended on the earth
and preached a heaven in the sky

he walked on the waters
he multiplied the bread
he sent the devil in the lake
and do not be surprised
he was instantly crucified

so he went up to see his dad
and said there is a way
to make things come to rest
give them just peace no guns
and they will stop the pray

IV.

after a while came the day
and the hour
jesus returned to his people

all americans saw him
descend
in his new white dress
against the blue sky
with many rays of gold
shining on his long waving hair
a little kitsch
and neo-gothic
but good enough
to be recognized by all
with his cross
as the king of kings

and lo! all americans heard
even the dead americans heard

the son of god say
with a voice like a clarinet
the last day has come
the last judgment
will start in a minute

and they all sung like angels
with the angels
and like saints
with the saints
and like virgins
with the virgins
and like rappers
with the rappers
and like x-actors
with the x-actors
the methodists
with the catholics
the baptists
with the lgbttqqiaap
the scientologists
with the seventh day adventists

the mormons
with the muslims
the new age
with the old age
the evangelicals
with the hell's angels
and all the sects in between
and even the atheists sang
like they had never sung before
a little out of tune but still

then the son of man
slightly floating above the earth
walking on air as if on water
opened his mouth
this time like a trumpet
pronouncing the word
hey! people
or hey! guys if you prefer
this is the universal judgment
you all prayed for
since you came to this land
centuries ago

come on white sheep
on my right
you know why and
come on black sheep
on my left
with no discrimination intended
the times haven't changed
since your fathers killed
the natives that welcomed them
therefore let us have a security check
before we go into the air
first you'll lay down your guns
at the feet of my father
who is your father too
our god
amen

here we saw an example of
how even a king of kings
can be misinformed
about his flock, his very own
flock

the president in his white house twittering
resumed the situation well when he
trumpeted back to jesus
christ! we prefer to be in hell
with our guns
than in heaven without them
so you get the hell out of here
and let us now pledge the pledge
applaud our veterans
and listen to that banner thing

so it happened
that the last day ended
as the first day began
it was a beautiful day
it was an unforgettable day
it was a new national holiday
jesus-christ gunday

More Guns

this year we celebrate
30,000 assassinations
(thirty thousand)
without counting police violence
(police violence?)
guns don't kill
says the rifle shop
indeed americans do
guns don't always kill
says the gun fair
indeed they hurt even more
but we don't count
the bruised lives
the troubled hearts

in 2015 between hanukkah and xmas
two americans

of the muslim creed
killed fourteen
compatriot americans
business as usual
freedom is its name
the american dream
equally for all
men and women and
what's in between
but surprise or no surprise
presidential candidates had
an orgasm in public
death to islam said one
all muslims must hang said another
kick them out don't let them in
carpet bomb their lands
one religion one billion terrorists
they said it in prayer
they said it in church
they said it in school
they said it on tv
they said it in a rally
they said it to the children
they said it to the grandparents

no one mentioned
29,986 other assassins
no creed indicated
without counting police violence
(police violence?)

username usa
password kill
kill for a constitution
kill for an amendment
kill at home

and can't you kill at home
then send the marines
to kill abroad
the navy the army the drones
kill in the desert
kill in the mountain
kill in the city
because the dead
the dead won't kill us at home

but americans will

Son of a Gun

There was an argument in heaven

Father and Son
Sitting on a greyish cloud

Said the Father to the Son
Son, it seems to be time to intervene
The farce has lasted long enough
Over there on our own earth
If that dirty cloud weren't here
I could show you where

Father, I know what you mean
Everyone knows
Don't lose your time explaining to me
I'm omniscient
You should know it since you are too.

Son, I don't think the farceur in charge
Deserves a war
He would become a hero
He would become so proud
Deserves not even a bomb on his own head
He would become a martyr.
Therefore this is my idea
Let's send some unknown germ
Brand-new virus from our vaults
You would help me find the right one
He is a tough fellow to fell
We gave him a lot of stamina
But the doctors would need time
The pharmaceutical industry is slow
The world would go berserk
And his enemies would be happy
And everybody is his enemy.

I know, Pa, I know stop
Stop patronizing your kids,
Or your kid in our case.
The case is historic if not hysteric
But you can learn something new.

Me?

Yes you. Even God can learn
Since you have to share
Your god-head with me
You're not one, got it?
We're both half of infinity.

Teach me your half then, Son.

My pleasure, Dad, look
You've created the earth all good
In your eyes
We respect you for it
But it doesn't work out that good
You see?

Hmm
Explain yourself
But don't try my patience or my pride
Or I won't see
And you know how catastrophic that can be

Shut it, Almighty, and look
The country you can't show me
Is an example of the law I will teach you.

What law! I *am* the law!

No! you speak of moral laws, and flaws,
I say statistics, you created them all
With a lot of other contradictions,
But then you forgot to honor them
You broke them
And we have to glue the pieces together
So keep your lips tight.

Tut tut!

Well, dear Father, imagine
A good man
On the throne of your country
Exactly one as you like it
And me too honestly
Exactly one you'd vote for
If you were not a resident alien.

Look however much he tries
However much he thinks speaks shows
However clearly he explains
Their problems to his people
His hard-headed stiff-necked but touching
people
And he argues and he proves
That two plus two equals four
And that the law is
To protect the weak and poor
He works hard for it
He does not even sleep at night
So we hope the best but
Now I tell you
Statistics, statistics will demonstrate
That powerful man is powerless
The good man can't undo the bad.

What Son? Your law isn't worth a dime
You don't need statistics to know that
Ha! I created the world…

Silence Father, wait! Now is given a bad man
On the throne, got it?

Bad in his heart
And vulgar in his mouth
And mean in his mind
And stupid to the bone
And says the law is to attack the poor
And to protect the rich
Exactly as you hate it
And me too honestly.
Alas! We can't do anything about it
We are trapped in our own nets
Democracy they call it.
One of those words!
But! Now statistics will prove
However much the bad man tries
And however much he cries and lies
And sleeps at night and often in the day
Or plays a silly game in the grass,
And you fear the worst
For the world and for us
Because without the world
We are nothing
Lo! However hard he tries
However hard he hires
The dumbest people at his side

And they try and they hire
Stupider and meaner
That powerful man is powerless
The bad man can't undo the good.

Son, dear Son, you speak in tongues
That no one can understand
You have not lived
Long enough and you are but a child
Or a student at a university.

Oh, no! Creator of all things (save me)
I know what you mean
I know the good men and the bad
I lived not that long but
Didn't they crucify me, you remember?
There are exceptions
But they confirm the rule
As there are rules
Confirming the exceptions
That is the case when you are god
haha!

Said the Father, Son,
Son now stop immediately
You make me so tired
With your eternal arguments
I will not interfere anymore
Since you interfere with me
I will let the earth alone
And on its own
Do the good
And the bad
Because
As such it was conceived
By me and more or less
By accident.

ONE DAY JESUS CHRIST

i.

one day jesus christ
in his well-known garb
walked into a town
peace to all he said
i am your lord
save your souls

they arrested him and said
you have no car
you have no license
you have no credit
you have no church
you have no gun

jesus christ responded no
there was a writing on the wall
there was a sign in heaven
there was a quaking of the earth
i am your lord and shepherd
believe me now and be saved

They said you're not from here
We are from here and
our souls are safe
we have no lord but ourselves
we need no shepherd
sheep we are not

To themselves they murmured
he makes me feel unsafe
he makes me feel insecure
if he looks like a terrorist
and he sounds like a terrorist
he must be a terrorist

we can frighten him
we can imprison him
we can mock him
we can scourge him
we can crown him with thorns
we can crucify him

jesus christ full of compassion spoke
you don't know what you're doing
my last words are for you
sit in paradise to my side
my spirit is in your hands
and my life belongs to you

they spoke between themselves
let there be justice
we have our laws
let us be constitutional
we have a second amendment
let us be ourselves

the die has been thrown
it is written that one man die
so that the people live
let the whole people decide
let all our nationals
take their lives in their hands

then there happened a miracle when
three hundred twenty
seven million three hundred
seventy-eight thousand
nine hundred and fifty
one guns fired like one

a cry was heard in town
a candle was lit at the courthouse
a flag was planted
the people wept at the local tv
between football and commercial
and all prayed like one

ii.

one day jesus christ
walked into a church
there was a lot to be seen
there was a lot to be heard
there was a lot to be prayed
and they went to their cars
they went home the faithful

they went home the faithful
they ate and they drank
the rich with the rich
the poor with the poor
the black with the black
the white with the white
the natives with the natives
the jews with the jews
the muslims with the muslims
the mormons with the mormons
the republicans with the republicans
the democrats with the democrats

jesus christ felt lonely in the church

iii.

(the gospel editor)

one day jesus christ
was hanging on the cross
edit: ~~on~~ at
edit: ~~at~~ from ~~the cross~~
a tree
it happened in Jerusalem
edit: Jerusalem, VA
edit: Jerusalem, ~~VA~~ MS
a roman soldier came by
edit: ~~roman~~ u s
edit: ~~soldier~~ veteran
edit: ~~veteran~~ police officer
upset
edit: ~~upset~~ afraid
edit: ~~afraid~~ alarmed
jesus was dying
edit: was ~~dying~~ not dead

edit: was ~~not dead~~ alive
he spoke seven words
edit: ~~seven words~~ a good word
edit: ~~good~~ hearty
edit: ~~hearty word~~ farewell speech
and jesus expired
edit: ~~jesus expired~~
and something went wrong
edit: ~~and something went wrong~~
presumption of innocence
edit: ~~presumption of innocence~~
no video no witnesses
it was a friday evening
edit: a good friday ~~evening~~
edit: a good old friday night
the man
edit: ~~man~~ man or woman
edit: ~~man or woman~~ person
took his
edit: his or her
edit: ~~his or her~~ their
Editor: their is more correct here!

Writer: but their is ...
wrong ... one *person*
Editor: it is correct
Writer: grammatically no!
Editor: politically yes!
their machine gun
edit: ~~machine~~ gun
edit: ~~gun~~ weapon of service
out of rage
edit: ~~rage~~ fear
edit: ~~fear~~ self-defense
and shot jesus in the heart
edit: ~~in the heart~~ in the chest
edit: ~~in the chest~~ in the belly
edit: ~~in the belly~~ in the legs
water and blood poured
edit: ~~water and~~ blood
~~poured~~ streamed
edit: ~~streamed~~ dripped
from the wounds
edit: ~~the wounds~~ a wound
edit: an alleged wound

the temple shook on its foundations
edit: ~~the temple~~ the Capitol
edit: ~~the Capitol~~ Congress
edit: ~~shook on its foundations~~
started an investigation

the autopsy shows jesus died from a
heart attack

iv.

One day Jesus Christ
decided to leave the earth
to its own judgment
like a tired parent lets
the teenager child
leave the house

But before his adieu
he would bless all creatures
preparing their fight
for survival of the fittest
a hell of a job
the blessing I mean

all animals had a chance
to pass before him
while he sat on the hill top
a long line longing & queuing
like a tape wrapping the globe
several times

And Jesus blessed like never before
in his entire life. Africa first,
and it made him cry; Asia &
Europe made him mad;
Antarctica made him cold;
Australia made him hot.

America was last but not least
with its cougars and red wolves
and more cats & dogs
the queue was the longest
since Noah's ark, this time
there was no ark.

When Jesus thought it was finally over
a bloodsucker fell from out of nowhere
on his white shoulder and it said
thanks for that blood of yours
but could you do me a favor though
I need a blessing too.

Not so fast answered the lord,
I hoped you would never show up
I heard everybody hates you
a little interrogation is needed
and get your teeth
out of my neck.

From all my creatures I've heard
you sucked the precious blood,
figuratively I mean.
Literally also, lord, was the answer
and I have fans who'd give
their life for me, literally too.

In fact, they know the deal
I suck their blood, the suckers!
btw, your blood is saving me
right now from eternal death
yes pardon me, your blood
for my redemption.

Then Jesus sighed: Aye, be it so
my blood will be your blood.
Without suckers the world
wouldn't be the world.
You'll be blessed in your bloody way,
Suck on, but I have to save my soul. Now!

v.

one day jesus christ
fell from his father's lap
accidents happen
in the divine world

and he was swallowed by
the maelstrom of the
gravitational fields
of galaxies and stars

a missing electron
absorbed in the orbit
of planet earth
nothing stopped his downfall

until he met a wandering cloud
and traveled with her
over deserts and oceans and
dripped with a raindrop in a

pool of stagnant water
full of larvae busy
becoming mosquitos male
and female searching for blood

and via the saliva of the insect
biting the innocent ear
of a maiden listening to the voice
of a radiant young man

jesus dove into her bloodstream
and swam with his little arms and legs
all the way to the warm womb
of that candid renaissance beauty

he had the best time of his life
growing fast in her bold bald belly
the virgin was petrified and
almost stoned for tradition's sake

she had to run for her life
to give birth in a stable
between ox and ass and hop
jesus sat on the lap of his mother

oh said the visiting shepherds
he will be a good shepherd
ah said the visiting kings
he will be a wise king

but the real king was furious
and killed all the real children
the holy family had better leave
the palestinian territory

like on the wings of silver birds
it was the famous flight to egypt
to alexandria more precisely but
oh error it was alexandria va

so jesus grew up in america
without apparent sin
but with many a hamburger and
he often changed water into coke

one day his mother and godfather
took him to the capital
a long and heavily delayed train ride
he was only twelve years old

well they lost him in the crowd
(he was only twelve years old)
looked for three days around the mall
he was only twelve years old

found him in the capitol
discussing with the reps
who said oh my god
this boy knows the law

his mother took him home
his godfather taught him
how to build a house but jesus
longed for the hill

he hitched along the highways
and he hiked in the towns
he told stories for a living
and read the future in a palm

only thirty-three years old
to the hill he returned and saw
nobody but bankers there
money money in the raw

this house he cried aloud
is our fathers' house he cried
not a robbers' den and he knocked
them all out with a golf club

he was sent to death
and stands in the death row now
the state can't find
the right amount of poison

did you ever hear of that
I didn't but jesus said
don't worry fellow men
when I'm dead I will come back

vi.

One day Jesus Christ
heard his father sigh
and it was not a hurricane
not a tornado
but more like the silence
before the storm
and Jesus wrote down a new word
in the stardust: sighlence.

Then he listened again and there
was a thought, his father's thought
of course (they were so verbally united!):
would Jesus once more
(only one more time)
(a short and little time)
go back to planet earth,
and see how it had changed?

Wouldn't he like to see his mother
how well she was doing and his old friends
and with fresh eyes his fatherland
its new leaders and the old temple
and the hill called Golgotha
where he had died and his tomb
he didn't lose his time in?
A real pilgrimage, indeed!

He could finally apologize
for having disappeared
so abruptly with hardly an explanation
leaving his disciples in big trouble
because of his very name
they would accept his excuses
they had also encountered
certain miraculous advantages.

He could even start over his mission,
one learns from one's mistakes.
There were more people now, more peoples
to convert, more sins to forgive,
more sick and blind and deaf to heal
and more poor to beatify,
more dead to raise,
more pharisees to chastise. So exciting!

Jesus had no time to think "no, never".
For God the present is already the past.
The future has taken place before it has started.
God had an idea in the back of his mind.
He didn't understand earth words anymore,
the terms they were a-changing.
Jesus could learn the new language and
update the dictionary. Wasn't he his Word?

So it happened, God's ideas are after all
The immediate form of reality.
A new incarnation was prepared. Where?
The Old World had disqualified itself.
Go for the New World where all things are new.
Was a virgin really necessary? Was that legal
With an aged man? Too risky! And a stable?
No! Replaced by a country resort hotel.
Shepherds neither. A farmer maybe on a
mowing machine?

Kings yes. With turbans and kaftans, plenty, in
limousines
Black and shiny as pasteurized petrol. Angels?
Fireworks were always a splendid finale, okay,
and
Songs for peace would never bother anyone.

What about a new carnal disguise? Female?
Black? Both?
A massacre of young innocents? To hit the news
on t.v.?
No problem: contact a terrorist.
And a splendid negro girl was born in
New Bethlehem.

About her life we can be short. She was
recognized
by none, not even by herself. But she loved the
poor and the impure
and the handicapped and the depressed
and the traumatized for life, she helped the junks
and the soldiers and the refugees and the
condemned to death,
she run for president, and running accused
the priests and the powerful and was shot.
Blood stained like an embroidered rose her
ripped blue jeans.

When Jesus returned, his or her father hardly
recognized her
Or him or them or it. No word suited anymore.
Traveling educates the young and old.
Listen to the homecoming discussion:
"What's the news, child? Fake, father, fake.
How are the leaders, kid? Misleaders, dad,
misleaders.
Are my people happy? Happy to be unhappy.
What about the truth? Truth is a lie, o eternal
papa!"

From the eternal papa's eye, a tear dropped
And it was not rain, not dew, not drizzle but
deluge.
It was a devastating flood, as he spoke
"Let us then destroy the people we made
With all our loving wisdom which now means
folly.
And according to my quantum calculations
We three should leap into a parallel eternity."
And all was quiet in the heavens.

Also by Jan Laurens Siesling in Just So Editions:

How the Rhino Lost its Horn & Other Just So Songs,
2019